A CENTURY *of*
LLANDUDNO

New Coastal Defences, West Shore, 1998.

A CENTURY *of* LLANDUDNO

JIM ROBERTS

This book was first published in 1999 by Sutton Publishing Limited

This new paperback edition first published in 2007 by Sutton Publishing

Reprinted in 2010 by
The History Press
The Mill, Brimscombe Port,
Stroud, Gloucestershire, GL5 2QG
www.thehistorypress.co.uk

Reprinted 2011

British Library Cataloguing in Publication Data
A catalogue record for this book is available from the British Library.

ISBN 978-0-7509-4936-1

Front endpaper: Llandudno Bay from the air, 1992.
Back endpaper: A busy Llandudno Promenade, 1997.
Half title page: Wild Goat – Great Orme.

*To my mother Vivian who, at 93 years of age, has witnessed these changes,
and to my grandchildren: Danielle, Zoë, Ben, Rebecca, Harry and Amy
who will witness many more.*

Title page: Promenade and Pier Pavilion, 1910.

A Walk on the Pier, *c.* 1905.

Typeset in Photina.
Typesetting and origination by
Sutton Publishing.
Printed and bound in Great Britain.

Contents

The Happy Valley was famous for its minstrel shows and here we see a group which was immensely popular before the First World War, Perry's Happy Valley Minstrels. During the day the troupe would 'busk' in the streets of the town to act as trailer to the main show in the valley. During the performance the wealthy, paying, audience sat in deck chairs at a few pence a time, but the majority watched from Aberdeen Hill. Another popular group was Churchill's Minstrels, whose leader Billy Churchill performed in the first Royal Command Performance in 1912. On Sundays, fervent nonconformist and evangelical meetings were held in the Happy Valley.

Britain: A Century
of Change

Children gathered around an early wireless set in the 1920s. The speed and forms of communication were to change dramatically as the century advanced. (*Barnaby's Picture Library*)

T he delirious rejoicing at the news of the Relief of Mafeking, during the Boer War in May 1900, is a colourful historical moment. But, in retrospect, the introduction that year of the first motor bus was rather more important, signalling another major adjustment to town life. In the previous 60 years railway stations, post-and-telegraph offices, police and fire stations, gas works and gasometers, new livestock markets and covered markets, schools, churches, football grounds, hospitals and asylums, water pumping stations and sewerage plants had totally altered the urban scene, as the country's population tripled and over 70 per cent were born in or moved to the towns.

When Queen Victoria died in 1901, she was measured for her coffin by her grandson Kaiser Wilhelm, the London prostitutes put on black mourning and the blinds came down in the villas and terraces spreading out from the old town centres. These centres were reachable by train and tram, by the new bicycles and still newer motor cars, connected by the new telephone, and lit by gas or even electricity. The shops may have been full of British-made cotton and woollen clothing but the grocers and butchers were selling cheap Danish bacon, Argentinian beef, Australasian mutton, tinned or dried fish and fruit from Canada, California and South Africa. Most of these goods were carried in British-built-and-crewed ships, burning Welsh steam coal.

As the first decade moved on, the Open Spaces Act meant more parks, bowling greens and cricket pitches. The first state pensions came in, together with higher taxation and death duties. These were raised mostly to pay for the new Dreadnought battleships needed to maintain naval superiority over Germany, and deter them from war. But the deterrent did not work. The First World War transformed the place of women, as they took over many men's jobs. Its other legacies were the war memorials which joined the statues of Victorian worthies in main squares round the land. After 1918 death duties bit even harder and a quarter of England changed hands in a few years.

Women working as porters on the Great Western Railway, Paddington, *c.* 1917. (*W.L. Kenning/ Adrian Vaughan Collection*)

The multiple shop – the chain store – appeared in the high street: Sainsburys, Maypole, Lipton's, Home & Colonial, the Fifty Shilling Tailor, Burton, Boots, W.H. Smith. The shopper was spoilt for choice, attracted by the brash fascias and advertising hoardings for national brands like Bovril, Pears Soap, and Ovaltine. Many new buildings began to be seen, such as garages, motor showrooms, picture palaces (cinemas), 'palais de dance', and the bow-windowed, pebble-dashed, tile-hung, half-timbered houses that were built as ribbon-development along the roads and new bypasses or on the new estates nudging the green belts.

During the 1920s cars became more reliable and sophisticated as well as commonplace, with developments like the electric self-starter making them easier for women to drive. Who wanted to turn a crank handle in the new short skirt? This was, indeed, the electric age as much as the motor era. Trolley buses, electric trams and trains extended mass transport and electric light replaced gas in the street and the home, which itself was groomed by the vacuum cleaner.

A major jolt to the march onward and upward was administered by the Great Depression of the early 1930s. The older British industries – textiles, shipbuilding, iron, steel, coal – were already under pressure from foreign competition when this worldwide slump arrived, cutting exports by half in two years and producing 3 million unemployed (and still rising) by 1932. Luckily there were new diversions to alleviate the misery. The 'talkies' arrived in the cinemas; more and more radios and gramophones were to be found in people's homes; there were new women's magazines, with fashion, cookery tips and problem pages; football pools; the flying feats of women pilots like Amy Johnson; the Loch Ness Monster; cheap chocolate and the drama of Edward VIII's abdication.

Father and child cycling past Buckingham Palace on VE Day, 8 May 1945. (*Hulton Getty Picture Collection*)

Things were looking up again by 1936 and unemployment was down to 2 million. New light industry was booming in the Home Counties as factories struggled to keep up with the demand for radios, radiograms, cars and electronic goods including the first television sets. The threat from Hitler's Germany meant rearmament, particularly of the airforce, which stimulated aircraft and aero engine firms. If you were lucky and lived in the south, there was good money to be earned. A semi-detached house cost £450, a Morris Cowley £150. People may have smoked like chimneys but life expectancy, since 1918, was up by 15 years while the birth rate had almost halved. The fifty-four hour week was down to forty-eight hours and there were 9 million radio licences by 1939.

In some ways it is the little memories that seem to linger longest from the Second World War: the kerbs painted white to show up in the blackout, the rattle of ack-ack shrapnel on roof tiles, sparrows killed by bomb blast, painting your legs brown and then adding a black seam

A family gathered around their television set in the 1950s. (*Hulton Getty Picture Collection*)

down the back to simulate stockings. The biggest damage, apart from London, was in the south-west (Plymouth, Bristol) and the Midlands (Coventry, Birmingham). Postwar reconstruction was rooted in the Beveridge Report which set out the expectations for the Welfare State. This, together with the nationalisation of the Bank of England, coal, gas, electricity and the railways, formed the programme of the Labour government in 1945. At this time the USA was calling in its debts and Britain was beggared by the war, yet still administering its Empire.

Times were hard in the late 1940s, with rationing even more stringent than during the war. Yet this was, as has been said, 'an innocent and well-behaved era'. The first let-up came in 1951 with the Festival of Britain and then there was another fillip in 1953 from the Coronation, which incidentally gave a huge boost to the spread of TV. By 1954 leisure motoring had been resumed but the Comet – Britain's best hope for taking on the American aviation industry – suffered a series of mysterious crashes. The Suez debacle of 1956 was followed by an acceleration in the withdrawal from Empire, which had begun in 1947 with the Independence of India. Consumerism was truly born with the advent of commercial TV and most homes soon boasted washing machines, fridges, electric irons and fires.

The *Lady Chatterley* obscenity trial in 1960 was something of a straw in the wind for what was to follow in that decade. A collective loss of inhibition seemed to sweep the land, as stately home owners opened up, the Beatles and the Rolling Stones transformed popular music, and retailing, cinema and the theatre were revolutionised. Designers, hairdressers, photographers and models moved into places vacated by an Establishment put to flight by the new breed of satirists spawned by *Beyond the Fringe* and *Private Eye*.

In the 1970s Britain seems to have suffered a prolonged hangover after the excesses of the previous decade. Ulster, inflation and union troubles were not made up for by entry into the EEC, North Sea Oil, Women's Lib or, indeed, Punk Rock. Mrs Thatcher applied the corrective in the 1980s, as the country moved more and more from its old manufacturing base over to providing services, consulting, advertising, and expertise in the 'invisible' market of high finance or in IT. Britain entertained the world with *Cats, Phantom of the Opera, Four Weddings and a Funeral, The Full Monty, Mr Bean* and the *Teletubbies*.

The post-1945 townscape has seen changes to match those in the worlds of work, entertainment and politics. In 1956 the Clean Air Act served notice on smogs and pea-souper fogs, smuts and blackened buildings, forcing people to stop burning coal and go over to smokeless sources of heat and energy. In the same decade some of the best urban building took place in the 'new towns' like Basildon, Crawley, Stevenage and Harlow. Elsewhere open warfare was declared on slums and what was labelled inadequate, cramped, back-to-back, two-up, two-down, housing. The new 'machine for living in' was a flat in a high-rise block. The architects and planners who promoted these were in league with the traffic engineers, determined to keep the motor car moving whatever the price in multi-storey car parks, meters, traffic wardens and ring roads.

Carnaby Street in the 1960s. (*Barnaby's Picture Library*)

The Millennium Dome at Greenwich, 1999. (*Michael Durnan/Barnaby's Picture Library*)

The old pollutant, coal smoke, was replaced by petrol and diesel exhaust, and traffic noise. Even in the back garden it was hard to find peace as motor mowers, then leaf blowers and strimmers made themselves heard, and the neighbours let you share their choice of music from their powerful new amplifiers, whether you wanted to or not. Fast food was no longer only a pork pie in a pub or fish-and-chips. There were Indian curry houses, Chinese take-aways and American-style hamburgers, while the drinker could get away from beer in a wine bar. Under the impact of television the big Gaumonts and Odeons closed or were rebuilt as multi-screen cinemas, while the palais de dance gave way to discos and clubs.

From the late 1960s the introduction of listed buildings and conservation areas, together with the growth of preservation societies, put a brake on 'comprehensive redevelopment'. Now the new risk at the end of the 1990s is that town centres may die, as shoppers are attracted to the edge-of-town supermarkets surrounded by parking space, where much more than food and groceries can be bought. The ease of the one-stop shop represents the latest challenge to the good health of our towns. But with care, ingenuity and a determination to keep control of our environment, this challenge can be met.

Llandudno: An Introduction

At the turn of the century Llandudno was coming to the end of a rapid expansion programme which had been carefully supervised by a team of Improvement Commissioners. This group of twenty men, appointed after the passing of the Llandudno Improvement Act of 1854, was largely responsible for the way the town looks to this day: a town of wide sweeping airy streets, with carefully designed buildings. The Commissioners' concern was the harmonious development of the town, and they supervised the provision of highways, drainage, sewage-disposal, water and gas, and also provided for law and order. In 1895 the responsibilities were handed over to the newly appointed Urban Council which has since developed and nurtured the town with much the same degree of care and attention. During its relatively short urban history the town has been acclaimed as the premier coastal resort of Wales, and it has justifiably earned the accolade, 'The Queen of Welsh Resorts'. The beautiful sweep of the bay as viewed from the Little Orme has led to it being called 'The Naples of the North'.

Before 1843 the Creuddyn Peninsula, on which the town is built, was a sparsely populated area with two magnificent bays, topped and tailed by two splendid headlands, the Great and Little Ormes. The flatland between the headlands was saltmarsh, desolate and windswept. Cottages were clustered under the Great Orme, from where the inhabitants made a meagre living from the sea, and from the quarries and copper mines on the headland, sheep were kept, and there were small farming ventures across the peninsula. The area was ripe for development.

During the past hundred and fifty years the influence of the Mostyn Estate on the development of Llandudno has been considerable. In 1843 Edward Mostyn MP introduced the Eglwysrhos, Llandudno and Llangystenin Enclosure Bill into Parliament. In 1848 the Apportionment Award was completed and the population could only look on as the area was neatly parcelled up and shared among its principal freeholders. Not surprisingly, the major share of 832 acres of the common land went to Edward Mostyn. The Lord Bishop of Bangor, the Right Revd Christopher Bethel, a staunch supporter of Edward Mostyn, was rewarded with 18 acres, and a sinecure rector got 5 acres. The people

Llandudno from Bryn Maelgwyn, *c.* 1860.

were given 1.5 acres and 30 square yards for digging a well. For this return they lost their rights to the common land, grazing, rabbit catching, hay-gathering and so on. It has been suggested elsewhere that this act robbed the people of Llandudno of their only asset. This was part of a nationwide epidemic of such Acts, and throughout Great Britain 6 million acres of open land were grabbed shamelessly by the perpetrators of 4,000 acts of parliament.

The combined efforts of the Mostyn Estate and Owen Williams, a Liverpool architect, led to the swift development of the Creuddyn. There was a rapid population increase as building and civil engineering projects got under way. The population in 1801 was a mere 381, and by 1851 this had trebled. By 1854 Mostyn Street and the Church Walk area were almost complete, and the seafront hotels were hard on their heels. St George's Hotel was built in 1854, the first of many to follow. The motive force for these projects was the vision of Owen Williams who had foreseen the attractions of the area for tourists, and the tailor-made opportunities to satisfy the increasingly widespread demands for watering places and holiday resorts.

The first pier was built in 1858, when proposals were made to turn Llandudno into 'Port Wrexham', a coal exporting, and packetboat harbour for links with Ireland. This proposed development went to the rival bidders, the mainline Chester & Holyhead Railway Company. As a result, North Wales' premier port became Holyhead. The first pier was destroyed in the Great Storm of 1859, and the present one was built in 1876–7. Marine Drive, around the Great Orme, was completed in 1878. In the 1870s the development moved slowly across the Bay towards the Little Orme and the Craig-y-Don area. The West Shore lagged behind the other parts of the town, and building went on here mainly after 1900, as it did in the Penrhyn Bay suburb of Llandudno. In 1858 the link with the mainline railway system at Llandudno Junction was made and this produced a significant increase in the number of visitors to the town.

Llandudno was one of the first products of the railway era. It became one of the most flourishing resorts along the North Wales coast, and it was the first whose development was carefully planned with tourism in mind. Initially the social make-up of the early visitors was mainly the middle and professional classes, but the introduction of cheap railway

Llandudno before the construction of the Pier, *c.* 1860.

Upper Mostyn Street, *c.* 1860.

fares and more frequent and faster trains meant that a wider social range from a wider area was able to avail itself of the seaside holiday. In the middle of the nineteenth century a visit to the seaside was becoming a must for everybody, cotton workers from Lancashire, iron workers from the Midlands, and potters from Staffordshire were making their annual pilgrimage, and the tourist industry expanded to cater for the demand. Most resorts, like Llandudno, were building promenades, and a walk on the 'prom' became a regular evening occurrence after dinner or high tea, with perhaps a visit to the bandstand or the pierrot show for some gentle entertainment. Many resorts were building piers, and a walk on the pier also became an obligatory activity, to fill the lungs with sea air, and experience the thrill of walking on water. Above all, there was a widely held popular belief that immersion in the sea, and the consumption of sea-water, was a health-giving process, especially as it became fashionable during the reigns of George III and George IV for the gentry and nobility to 'take the waters' at Brighthelmstone

(Brighton), Weymouth and Eastbourne, and similar resorts. To satisfy increasing demands, new types of cheaper boarding establishments, bed and breakfast, and self-catering were built, with further to walk to the sea, and without the sea views.

The development of an efficient transport system is in itself causing a reduction in certain sectors of the tourist trade. Rapid and easy access, by definition, means rapid and easy egress. In Llandudno's case the building of the A55 link with the M6 and the major motorways has been of particular significance and, as a result, there has been a relative reduction in the number of people staying in the resort, and an increase in the number of day-trippers and short stay visitors. Being able to travel further, faster, cheaper, also means that the resorts of the Mediterranean, for instance, are available to everyone, and include sunburn as part of the package. This must be regarded as a major challenge, so that men and women, 'making temporary retreats from business in order to return with fresh vigour of body and mind, to the duties of their station' will choose Llandudno.

Llandudno distinguishes itself not only as a tourist resort: it also claims to be 'The Queen of North Wales Shopping Centres'. Since its early days, Mostyn Street, like Lord Street in Southport, has attracted good quality shops. In more recent years national chains have recognised the central role Llandudno plays in North Wales' consumer society. Marks & Spencer's arrival in 1936, and its development since, has proved a significant boost to the town's economy. This single large store draws people into the town from all over North Wales, and the knock-on effect for other town shops cannot be overestimated. The Improvement Commissioners, however, would not have approved of the architectural discord produced by its modern shop front. In more recent years, shopping in the area has followed the national pattern of out-of-town centres with supermarkets and superstores built on the edge of the town. This has produced the inevitable 'sameness' to the town fringes, as the superstore clones are put into place uniformly and mechanically. The town's Victoria Centre, opened in 1992, is a more imaginative project with decent architecture, and a much needed car park.

There are some who see a conflict between the town as a resort and the town as a shopping centre. This is rather a short-sighted view. There is no reason why it should not develop both of these functions harmoniously. There have been expressed misgivings about the deterioration of tourist facilities, and certain areas of dereliction within the town's confines, so-called 'brown sites', which cry out for development. With a modicum of good intention, and the appropriate financial means, there is no reason why these obvious problems should not be resolved as another century turns.

An unusual attraction on the Promenade at the turn of the century was this giant telescope. It must be said that our Victorian and Edwardian forebears were fascinated by the scientific, and at this time it was possible to experience the wonders of electricity at a show at the end of the pier. Moving picture shows (American Bioscopes) were also available in the basement of the Pier Pavilion. Part of the scientific was the Lantern Slide Show and this photograph was taken for lantern slide projection.

Setting the Scene

Knowledge of Llandudno's link with its prehistoric past was given a significant boost by the discovery of a pile of prehistoric remains in 1879, when this man, Thomas Kendrick, opened up the back of his workshop to extend it. The evidence accumulated during this find, and the discovery of so many prehistoric relics on the slopes of the Orme, confirm the habitation of the Orme from the Upper Paleolithic period through to the New Stone Age. 'Beaker' pottery 3,000 years old and Bronze Age tools have been found in recent times. The opening up of the copper mines and the exciting finds that ensued were of great significance. The Great Orme as a historical site has excited the interest of national as well as local historians. The Llandudno Historical Society and the Great Orme Exploration Society work ceaselessly and rigorously to gather information about this site of world importance.

St Tudno's Church photographed by Francis Bedford, *c.* 1870. It all began here in the seventh century when a hermit monk, the son of a chieftain whose lands had been swallowed by the sea, settled on the Orme and established a religious sanctuary. He was elevated to sainthood and was known as St Tudno. 'Llan' is Welsh for 'place' or 'enclosure' and so by linguistic gymnastics 'The Place of St Tudno' became 'Llandudno'. A church of some sort has existed here since before the year 1100, and parts of the present building have been dated to before 1400.

Owen Williams and Lord Mostyn are reputed to have met in 1844 in the hut seen here to map out the proposed development of the area as a watering place and holiday resort. This is an early photograph from about 1865. There is no pier, which was built jutting out to sea almost from this spot in 1877. The photograph has an added historic interest in that the boat being launched behind the crowd is believed to be the *Sister's Memorial* lifeboat which operated from the shore between 1861 and 1867.

he town grew outward
ross the bay from the Great
rme to the Little Orme. In
is engraving we can clearly
e this development. The
otels, starting with the St
eorge (1854) are beginning
hug the curvature of the
ay, and grand houses and
usiness premises are being
uilt in the Church Walks and
pper Mostyn Street areas.

everal years have passed, and in this photograph of about 1875 taken by the great Victorian photographer Francis Bedford
e can see the plans drawn up by Owen Williams beginning to take shape. Prince Edward Square (Triangle!) is there in
mbryo, and the roof configurations of North Parade are of interest. The emphasis Williams placed on the need for a wide
romenade is evident. In the background there is no development of any kind on the West Shore.

21

The only way around the Great Orme was a crude footpath hewn out of the cliff face, known as Cust's Path. Cust was a local solicitor who instigated the building of the path. It was a hazardous trip around the Orme, to say the least. In 1871 parliamentary permission was sought, and given, for the construction of a permanent way to replace the path. This was completed in 1875, and in the process of construction Llandudno lost some of its prehistoric past when several megalithic tombs were removed. The town council purchased the drive from the Marine Drive Company for £11,000 in 1897.

This very early view on the Great Orme shows the rough track later replaced by a metalled road and the tram track. The early inhabitants of the Orme probably used the track to attend worship at St Tudno's Church. In the eighteenth and early nineteenth century miners would have walked to the copper mines along this track.

As the turn of the century approaches, the town is beginning to take the shape we are familiar with. In this view from the Orme, behind Church Walks, taken about 1890, we can see that St George's Church has been built to replace the inconveniently situated, and too small, St Tudno's. This is to cater for the increasing town population and seasonal visitors. There are a half-dozen or so graves in the churchyard. The spires of the Nonconformist chapels are pricking the skyline, and the Hydro tower is visible on the promenade.

he portico of Zion Baptist Chapel is the prominent feature in a very early Mostyn Street with hardly a shop in sight. The hapel was built in 1862 and this photograph was taken not long after its completion. The unmetalled road surface must ave been a trial in muddy wet or dusty dry conditions. Llandudno was one of the first towns to experiment with a tar overing to cope with these problems. A considerable amount of reconstruction of the lower storeys of the buildings ccurred before Mostyn Street became the premier shopping street of North Wales.

The Happy Valley Theatre, at its earliest, is seen in this early Bedford photograph, a simple tent from which a husband an wife team entertained as 'Nigger Minstrels'. The previous entertainer at this venue was a promenade band conducted by Mr Round. From the 1870s the Happy Valley has been associated with 'minstrel'-type entertainment. Ironically, there is mo theatre in this photograph than there is in the Happy Valley today.

Building on Firm Foundations

Lot Williams sits outside his camera obscura which he had built in 1860 on what became known as Camera Hill. The ingenious contraption projected views on to a table from an arrangement of lenses in the turret. It stayed on the hill for over a century before it was torched by vandals in 1966. There is still an obscura there, built by a local man wishing to maintain a tradition.

Llandudno is fortunate in that it has two excellent beaches at its disposal. The North Shore with its attendant promenade is popular. The West Shore with spectacular sea views is quieter. To be at the seaside means to be on the beach, but, in Victorian and Edwardian Britain, it was considered infra dig to be brown and sunburned; this was the mark of the outdoor working class and the rustic peasant. Beach-going as an activity, therefore, was to be approached with care and the maximum protection. Photographs of beach scenes show people wearing a surprisingly large amount of clothing and carrying open parasols to ward off the offending rays.

This photograph is so typical of life on Llandudno beach in 1900 that it had to be included. It purports to be the 'Ladies' Bathing Place'. Mixed bathing was not allowed by law, and there was a 200-yard gap between the segregated areas. An incursion into that area cost a gentleman (or lady) a fine of £2. In 1894 the council relented somewhat, and allowed family bathing from a short stretch of beach near the Arcadia. The bathing machines at the water's edge are there to put a stop to nude bathing.

ladies and children, but no gentlemen, mean we are still in the ladies' bathing area. There are fewer clothes than normal, and pantaloons and upheld skirts allow for the obligatory paddle. Surprisingly some of the children are bare-headed. This is a charming group photograph.

Bathing machines provided a living for several generations of certain families in Llandudno. In the early years of sea-bathing, nudity was fairly common at the seaside. The machine (box on wheels) was hired for 6d, and the occupant changed into a bathing costume in the machine, and then, when ready, waved a flag through a hole in the wall. The machine was horse-drawn into the sea an appropriate distance until the water was sufficiently deep to obviate any chance of indecent exposure, and the bather was allowed 40 minutes bathing. The machines were still in evidence until 1958.

One family responsible for saving 85 lives must qualify that family for an entry in the *Guinness Book of Records*. They were a bathing machine proprietors on Llandudno's beach in the early years of the century. Samuel Edwards (1862–192?) (30 lives), his brother Robert (20 lives) and his son William (35 lives) were members of this family, and the people they save were all in danger of drowning. Samuel also pulled a ditched aeroplane out of the sea with his trusty steed, to the delight and admiration of a watching crowd. Samuel is offering advice to the young lady emerging from the sea, and below, whe he was in his later years, he is giving a child a ride on his bathing machine horse.

andudno promenade, 30 yards wide and about a mile and half long, represents quite an extensive area for promenading ith the family. The stretched legs and fresh sea air induce an appetite for high tea. There are seats the whole length of the romenade, so, if you get tired, you simply sit and watch the other promenaders. The Improvement Commissioners ensured the peace and tranquillity of the promenade by passing a by-law which forbids trading of any sort on the sea front. andudno holiday-makers are thus spared the sometimes brash commercialism that is a feature of so many other resorts.

his is an interesting view of a feature peculiar to Llandudno promenade. The structure with the conical roof in the reground is 'The Juggernaut'. This was a wheeled bandstand which could be moved, pulled by horses, to various places on the promenade as the need arose.

29

Two families shared the space available for traditional donkey rides on the beach. An agreed boundary was never transgressed by the donkeys, even though they changed from one side to the other on alternate days.

Strolling promenaders are approaching the pier entrance ready for another of Llandudno's attractions, a walk along the pie In the centre 'Professor' Codman is performing 'the old tragedy' Punch and Judy. The young trees in the foreground a nowadays succumbing to Dutch Elm disease, and are having to be removed.

In its early history there was a toll imposed to walk the pier. It cost 4*d*, and this was to defray the cost of construction, which was £25,000. At the pier entrance a variety of attractions were advertised such as the bill of fare at the Pier Pavilion, and carriage trips in 'rubber wheeled' conveyances. Today this is still the most congested part of the promenade, because the laws concerning trading are relaxed here, and ice cream, candy-floss, and suchlike are available.

he pier reaches out 2,295 ft into the sea, and was opened in 1877, the second pier to have been built on this spot. Brunlees esigned and supervised the construction of it; he also designed the piers at Rhyl and Southport. The ornamental ironwork ere, as elsewhere in the town, is an attractive feature which the town conservationists are anxious to preserve.

31

This is the front of the beautiful pier pavilion with its exemplary wrought-iron decoration, for many years the cultural cent of Llandudno, and North Wales. The great singers and orchestras performed here, conducted by such luminaries as Malco Sargent, Sir Adrian Boult and Thomas Beecham. The resident orchestra was conducted by an eccentric named Jules Riviè who was said to have taught Sir Henry Wood. He had a flamboyant and emotional temperament, which led to frequent row and to his eventual departure to conduct an orchestra on Colwyn Bay pier.

The pier serves a useful function in that passengers can embark and disembark directly from the larger steamships which began to visit Llandudno to bring in visitors from Liverpool and the Lancashire coast. They also provided a sea excursion service with pleasure trips along the coast and around Anglesey, and less frequent trips to the Isle of Man. The funnel of the steamer, probably *La Marguerite* can be seen behind the pier buildings as people prepare to embark, 1908.

he rocky, rugged terrain and extreme weather conditions mean that farming on the Orme is not an easy task, and the ᴴancial returns are not very good either. Consequently farmers and their wives look to the tourists for extra income during ᴴe season. This is Penymynydd Isa, *c.* 1910, now known as White Farm, and the sign on the door reads, 'Refreshments, ᴴda, milk, lemonade, teas'. There are hundreds of sheep roaming the Orme, and the unleashed dog seen here would not be ᴴ welcome sight to the farmer.

Just below the summit of the Orme is the old mining village with its spoil heaps and ventilation shafts. The wall covered shaft is 'Vivian's Shaft' which sank over 500 ft to below the level of the sea. This area was the principal mining area during the eighteenth and nineteenth centuries. Amazing discoveries were made here later, as will be seen. Despite the extensive evidence of mining activity in this photograph taken around 1910, mining had long since ceased.

The semaphore station on the Orme was built in 1827, and rebuilt and extended in 1841. It served as a means of sending messages to Liverpool from Holyhead through a relay of stations: the nearest to Llandudno was on Puffin Island. It might be thought that this was a long and troublesome technique – but far from it; a message sent from Holyhead could, through observation of swinging arms on masts, reach Liverpool some four minutes later. In the late 1840s the station ceased to function and was replaced by electricity. At the turn of the century the buildings were demolished as seen below, and the site was used for the new Great Orme Complex.

In this 1905 view there has been considerable development in Mostyn Street. The front of Ebenezer Chapel is to the left, and the houses opposite have now been provided with shop fronts. A tree was planted in 1877 in the forecourt of the chapel to commemorate the first wedding conducted there. It survived the demolition of the chapel in 1967, and the front of the new Victoria Shopping Centre was modified to cater for its spreading branches, but not long afterwards (1997) it was claimed by Dutch Elm disease.

pper Mostyn Street was where the street began its development, c. 1900. The building at the top is the Italian Warehouse, andudno's first supermarket. It was owned by Thomas Williams, who later moved to Hooson's Corner. He published a omplete Guide to Llandudno. On the right is one of the town's earliest post offices.

'Llandudno – The Queen of Welsh Watering Places' is the proclamation on the wall of the Domestic Bazaar Company, central in this photograph. This shop is one of the forerunners of the early Woolworth's principle 'everything for sixpence'. The Domestic Bazaar went one better and a shop sign in the same position in another photograph claims everything in the shop costs 6½d. The building to the right, behind the trees, belonged to the church, and was demolished in 1936.

A view from the North Western Hotel over North Western Gardens and down Mostyn Street. At this time the gardens we owned by the hotel, and they were sold to the council a little before 1920. Public toilets were built beneath the gardens the 1920s. George Robert Thompson, 'The Postcard King', has a shop mid-left in the photograph. He produced hundreds different photographic postcards of the area, some of which are included in this book. Horse traffic predominates, though tl tram tracks are in evidence.

art of the Gogarth Abbey Hotel, *c.* 1960, on the West Shore was once Pen Morfa, the home of Dean Liddell and family hose daughter Alice was the inspiration for the *Alice in Wonderland* and *Through the Looking Glass* stories of Lewis Carroll. he Liddell family had holidayed in Llandudno in 1861 when they stayed in the famous St Tudno Hotel near the Pier ead. In 1862 they had another holiday in the St George Hotel. Dean Liddell loved the town, and eventually purchased enmorfa (End of the Marsh or Shore) in August 1862. The family came to the town on high days and holidays for the ext ten years. The Dean would return to his academic duties at Oxford leaving his family in the town to continue rolonged vacations. When she was 81 years of age, Alice (Mrs Alice Hargreaves) wrote, '. . . I still have the happiest iemories of Penmorfa . . . and the rambles over the Great Orme and among the sand hills. I wish I could be present in erson to express my gratitude for those joyous days, and for the days I spent with Mr Dodgson'. This letter was in ssponse to an invitation she had received to be present at the unveiling of an Alice in Wonderland memorial on the West hore. It is a pity she was unable to attend; it might have put an end to many years of speculation about the hypothetical nks between Lewis Carroll and Llandudno.

This is the view on the West Shore about ninety years ago, with an Edwardian family at the boating pool. The white cottages in the background were built in 1783 during a revival in the copper industry, and there was a need for houses for copper miners. The toll-house at the end of the Marine Drive is to the left of the cottages, beyond the Gogarth Abbey Hotel, and above them is Invalid's Walk, a gently sloping incline to Haulfre Gardens. The fresh water in the boating pool comes from the old copper mine's drainage system.

This photograph probably dates from the early 1920s; housing development in this part of the town was later than elsewhere. The building on the right is still under construction, with an incomplete roof. The jetty on the shore in the background has now gone, and a promenade and sea wall has been built between the boating-pond and the beach.

One family dominated the entertainment life of the promenade for well over 100 years. This was the Codman family, the famous puppeteers. In 1864 Richard Codman arrived in Llandudno in a gypsy caravan. His horse died so the impoverished Richard gathered some driftwood from the beach and carved his puppets: the famous Punch and Judy sagas had arrived in Llandudno. The Improvement Commissioners were not too pleased and tried to have him stopped, but Codman fought back, and the rest is history. Thomas Codlin in *The Old Curiosity Shop* is a puppet master, and it is said that Charles Dickens drew upon Richard Codman for his portrayal of this character. Richard Codman's heir, the stalwart 'Professor' John Codman, ran the promenade show for forty years, and never missed a show. He died in 1980.

The antics of performing birds delighted the Victorian and Edwardian crowds on the promenade. The star of the show was the trainer, an ebullient performer, Mr Giciano Ferrari. A cockatoo flew around the Grand Hotel and returned to the table on his command, others pulled wagons and walked tightropes. Sometimes they decided to have a rest in the branches of the nearby trees, ignoring the ranting of their trainer, and this became a much-loved part of the act. He came to Llandudno at the turn of the century from Italy by way of Brighton. He, like so many before and after him, grew to love the town, and he lived here till he died in 1923. The photograph below gives some idea of the crowds Mr Ferrari could attract in 1911. Today the local council would probably not give permission for this type of entertainment on the promenade.

e Happy Valley was famous for its
nstrel shows, and above we see a
upe that performed here for many
ars before the First World War –
urchill's Minstrels. In the first Royal
ommand Performance in history, Billy
urchill entertained the King and Queen
1912. The wealthy, paying audience
t in deck chairs during the
rformance; the majority watched from
erdeen Hill as seen in the foreground.
eir enjoyment of the entertainment
as marred by constant attempts to avoid
e 'bottler', the man who walked among
em with the collecting box. Below is
other troupe of entertainers who were
re at the turn of the century, Perry's
appy Valley Minstrels.

At the turn of the century the horse reigned supreme on the streets of Llandudno. Large numbers of the townsfolk were involved in supporting this means of getting people and goods from one place to another. The cab trade parked on central Mostyn Street, in Upper Mostyn Street, at the railway station, and alongside the Grand Hotel for the pier trade. Like so many other businesses in the town, the work was seasonal and the winter months were lean ones.

xcursions and sight-seeing tours were
dvertised all over the town, and
utside the George Hotel we see a four-
-hand with possibly a day trip in
ont of it, 1910. From Llandudno to
wallow Falls in the rubber-wheeled
'Rocket' cost 7 shillings. A bigger
ehicle called the 'Prince of Wales' left
landudno at 8.45 a.m., arrived for
offee or a light lunch at Betws y Coed
t 11.15 a.m., and then went on to the
ountains of Snowdonia. A full day
rip on rather uncomfortable seats on
nmetalled roads was something that
ayed in the memory. Below, the
ansom cab with its top-hatted driver
s at the top of Mostyn Street, heading
wards Headlands Hill.

On 19 October 1907 the first official tram run occurred from the tram station on the West Shore to the terminus in Colwyn Bay. The service provided a valuable link between the communities separated by the Little Orme. Penrhyn Bay was little developed at this time, and Rhos-on-Sea was a small fishing village with tourist potential. The photograph shows tramcar no. 14 in Mostyn Street on the inaugural run. The opening seems to have attracted very little attention. This was the beginning of a service, which lasted for 49 years.

This view dates from soon after the tramway opened, *c.* 1908. This is the wide and airy (sometimes too airy) Gloddaet Street which runs between the two shores. The tram is on its way back to the terminus. The traffic is all horse-drawn, th motor car has not yet appeared, but it is not far away. In the bay *La Marguerite* is leaving the pier head, probably on her wa back to Liverpool.

The screech and squeal of tram wheels on steel track was a constant source of annoyance to the people who lived and worked near the sweep of track from Gloddaeth Street into Mostyn Street. In 1911 a councillor described the noise as being 'like the screeching of Kilkenny cats'. Complaints to the tramway company led to the rails being liberally greased, a road hazard not to be recommended to crossing pedestrians, or wheeled vehicles. Here there are two trams at the offending corner on a passing loop. The absence of traffic here at what appears to be midday, bears no comparison to today's congested conditions.

Two trams are on a passing loop at the top of the Bodafon fields stretch of the track. This area was known as Sunnyside or Sunny Hill. The furthest tram, coming up the hill, will soon be on the shelf that takes it down the Little Orme incline into Penrhyn Bay. There has been a considerable amount of house-building here since this time, and Mostyn Estates wish to develop it further, a move that is being vociferously contested by many local people.

Welsh people generally have a high regard for the value of education; Wales' second greatest export was teachers when the first was coal. An essential part of the Welsh community is the library, and the early miners set up institutes which provided library facilities throughout South Wales. Llandudno's first library was built next to the Zion Baptist church, which had been built ten years earlier. The first library was demolished and rebuilt on the same site in the first decade of this century, and was opened by Lord Mostyn on 15 September 1910.

The Town Hall, a well-proportioned and attractive building in Lloyd Street, was eight years in the planning and construction. The original plans, submitted in 1894, won the architect T.B. Silcock a £50 prize. It was built by Luther Roberts, and the fact that the cost of building doubled during the period of construction caused a great deal of ill-feeling, much of which was expressed in the council's inaugural meeting.

Water Street on the Great Orme derives its name from the ancient well and steam-pump that used to be situated there. The pump was used to pump water into a reservoir in the Happy Valley in the mid-nineteenth century. The supply of water on the Orme was a constant problem. The porosity of the limestone substrata meant that water was easily absorbed, and did not stay on the surface for very long. Springs appear lower down where soft limestone meets older and harder rocks. Several early photographs feature the water boys with their donkeys and churns. They provided a valuable service to the inhabitants of the Orme while earning a living for themselves. In this very rare photograph of about 1910, the boys are outside the 'Great Orme's Head post office'; it is now a dwelling house.

The summit of the Great Orme, c. 1920. This complex replaced the semaphore station in 1909. It was built as a Telegraph hotel by Thomas McDonald and was a relay station for shipping signals from Point Linas, Anglesey to Merseyside. An eighteen-hole golf course adjoined the buildings, and close inspection of this photograph shows people on the eighteenth green.

This is the longest funicular railway in Great Britain and it transports holiday-makers from Llandudno to the summit of the Great Orme. It opened on 31 July 1902. This photograph shows the half-way station on the day of the system's opening and the assembled men are the directors and workers on the line. The distance between the Victoria station and the summit is so great that the journey has to be completed in two stages. Between July and the end of September 1902 it had carried approximately 70,000 passengers to the half-way station. The top half of the line was opened in July 1903.

There are two trams on the passing loop at the less steep part of the route on the way to the summit. The passengers have change trams at the half-way station, which can be seen in the background. Steam power is used to drive two colliery-typ winding engines. Smoke from the winding station comes from the coal-burning boilers. The system used in excess of 25 tons of coke per year before being converted to electricity.

ying its trade from the pier in 1900 along with three other main boats was the *St Tudno II*, an elegant paddle-steamer, which could carry over 1,000 passengers on her three decks. The ship was ten years old at the turn of the century and until 1922 she brought tourists into the town and provided excursions around Anglesey. During the First World War she was a troopship, and in 1922, four years after her return to the North Wales coast, she was broken up.

The *St Elvies*, seen here in the Menai Strait, came to the North Wales coast in 1896. She was 567 tons gross with a speed of 18½ knots. She carried slightly fewer passengers than the *St Tudno II*. In 1915 she was requisitioned for wartime duties as a mine-sweeper and returned a year after the cessation of hostilities. In 1930 she was sold and broken up for scrap.

Snowdon was built by the Laird Brothers of Birkenhead in 1892 for the Snowdon Passenger Steamship Company Ltd of Liverpool. In 1899 the Liverpool and North Wales Steamship Company took over the Snowdon Company and acquired *Snowdon* She is the smallest sister of the fleet and could only carry just over 250 passengers. During the war she too worked as a mine-sweeper, from Dover to Harwich. She returned to North Wales in 1919, and in 1931 she was broken up.

La Marguerite stole everyone's heart. She was large, elegant and powerful with supremely comfortable amenities and was the pride of the North Wales fleet. She worked the Thames for a while, but arrived in North Wales in 1904. She could carry over 2,000 passengers. In the photograph she is passing through the strait between Anglesey and Puffin Island. She served as troopship during the war and many a poor soul took his last look at his homeland from her decks. She was superseded by *Tudno III* in 1926 and was broken up at Briton Ferry. There were days when she carried 1,000 day-trippers into Llandudno.

'Your Country Needs You' was Lord Kitchener's exhortation in 1914, and men volunteered in their thousands to face the 'dreaded Hun'. The photographs on this page are probably the saddest in the book. They show two recruitment parades in Mostyn Street. In the top picture the parade is led by a sailor twirling a flag creating an entirely inappropriate carnival atmosphere. Below the town band is playing a rousing march. Both activities were designed to reduce the dramatic intensity of the event, and cloud judgement. The parades would end in meetings where patriotic speeches by politicians, who were staying safely at home, urged young men to volunteer for the fields of France. Bob Owen (see p. 53) remembers these parades and was sixteen when he lied to get into the army.

A First World War tank was presented to the town in memory of the fallen. Its arrival was greeted with a great deal of excitement, and a parade was held through the streets. It was presented in 1922, and after a brief nine-year stay on the Marine Drive the council decided to get rid of it. It took a Manchester scrap firm a week to demolish the indestructible machine, and they were charged £1 for the scrap.

This postcard was printed during the First World War and posted in 1917. It is included in this selection of First World War photographs because of the message written on the back. It reads, 'My dear boy has had a marvellous escape, and is now a prisoner of war in German hands.' This sad comment, rejoicing in what can only be described as tragic, was made because the lady who wrote the card must have been aware of conditions in the trenches. One only hopes that he (her dear boy) made it to 1918 and after.

Sadly, in 1999, one of Llandudno's oldest and most respected residents died. Robert Owen was 99 years old, and his life had been closely linked with the town's development for almost a century. He was also the town's last living First World War hero. He fought in the trenches as a machine-gunner in the South Wales Borderers. At seventeen he was the youngest gunner in the regiment. (The photograph dates from the early 1920s.) The experiences he recounted to the author during years of friendship stretched the bounds of credibility. He and five friends arrived in France on a Thursday, and by the following Sunday four of them had been shot. There was no false bravado about Bob; he freely admitted that he was terrified most of the time he spent in the trenches, coping with death, disease and marauding rats. Conversations with Bob were laced with humour, and deep human understanding. When he was approaching his ninety-seventh birthday, he was interviewed by a raw young reporter who unthinkingly observed, 'I don't think I want to live to be ninety-seven'. Bob's reply was, 'You will when you are ninety-six'. The conclusions he drew about the First World War were typically his: 'If it happens again I think we should send the politicians'. During the latter years of his life he was interviewed on radio and television several times. His wartime reminiscences are recorded and held in the Imperial War Museum.

Sunlight No. 1 was sponsored by Lever Brothers of Port Sunlight the soap manufacturers. She arrived in Llandudno on 15 October 1887 after the *Sister's Memorial* left the service. *Sunlight* completed her last effective rescue in September 1897, and left the service in 1902 when the boat below arrived at Llandudno. In her time she saved the lives of 26 people.

The *Theodore Price* arrived in Llandudno in 1902, and she had a special significance for the people of the town since she wa designed and built largely to specifications drawn up by three of her crew: Coxswain John Hughes, Deputy Cox John Willian and crew member John Owen (who later became coxswain and a recipient of the RNLI medal). She was a ten-oar self-rightin boat and cost £908. She had a distinguished career and was responsible for saving the lives of 36 people in 42 major call-outs.

54

The people shown here in 1910, and many thousands like them down the years, have been the reason for Llandudno's progress and prosperity during the last century. They are the staff of the St George Hotel, the first hotel to be built on the promenade in 1854. The face-to-face contacts between the guests and the workers in the hotels are of crucial importance in the success, or otherwise, of a holiday, and it is probably true to say that the people represented by the group here have been undervalued over the years. Multiply this number by the number of large hotels, and add to it the hundreds of smaller establishments in and around the town, and it represents a substantial amount of employment, albeit of a temporary and seasonal nature.

Llandudno Swifts, 1900. The first reported football match in the area took place in 1875 when Llandudno lost 2–1 to Conway. Gloddaeth Rovers, formed in 1880, were the first team of any significance in the town. Their goal-keeper Hersee, a Llandudno hotelier, kept goal for Wales. The Swifts (a plebeian bunch) merged with Gloddaeth Rovers in 1891, and became a very strong team. In their time they played and beat Liverpool and Wolverhampton Wanderers. They later drew with Everton. They had a proud and proven record and won many Welsh Senior cups in the early years of the century.

The Edwardian age came to an end in 1910 with the death of Edward VII. George V came to the throne in that year and reigned until 1936. This is a 1910 photograph taken by Rickets of Llandudno, and published as a postcard. The crowds have gathered in the Happy Valley to hear that George V had been proclaimed king. This proclamation scene was repeated in all the major public places in Great Britain on this day.

Following the proclamation came the coronation, and the crowds have once again gathered in Happy Valley to hear the news. George had been Prince of Wales since 1901. He and Queen Mary were well-loved monarchs who ruled a country which went through momentous changes during their 26-year reign: First World War, General Strike, the Union of South Africa, among others.

56

6 August 1910 the first aeroplane to land in Wales landed on the Rhos-on-Sea golf course in the Penrhyn Bay suburb of
ndudno. An actor, W.G. Lorraine (aka Robert Jones) had flown over from Blackpool intending to land in Holyhead, and
m thence he hoped to fly on to Ireland. The Farman biplane had landed miles from its destination, but the flight of 63
es over the sea had set a record. Later, after several minor mishaps, Lorraine crashed at Llanfair-yng-Nghornwy in
glesey – the first aeroplane to crash in Wales. He eventually made it to Ireland on 11 September 1910, but had to swim
ore after ditching the aeroplane, which had run out of fuel.

Aeroplanes, in 1914, caused quite a bit of excitement wherever they went. The *Daily Mail* seaplane arrived in Llandudno July of that year and the crowds are here to get a closer look. The plane offered flights around the Orme, but the cost of was too much for most people.

The Queen of Welsh Resorts

A pleasant stroll, or an exciting drive: either way, the traveller is guaranteed views of towering limestone rocks and turbulent sea to remind him how adventurous such a journey would have been before the Marine Drive was built. Prime Minister Gladstone had to be led over some sections blindfolded because the view to the seas below the precipitous cliffs was so terrifying.

Two general views of the town taken in the mid-1930s demonstrate the extent of its development since the beginning of th century. There are still bathing machines on the beach – these did not disappear until 1958. In 1951 the film of Arno Bennett's novel *The Card* was made, and some scenes were filmed on Llandudno beach, with the bathing machines as feature. Below, the fields in the middle distance are waiting development, and a great deal of in-filling will occur in the ne few decades.

Another view along the promenade, with a difference from earlier views. The 'juggernaut' has gone, and there is now a permanent bandstand on a platform jutting from the promenade over the beach. The photograph is from the early 1940s but the bandstand was built in the mid-1920s.

This is Craig y Don, which developed a little later than the main town. Craig y Don is a very pleasant self-contained area, and the people of this part of town are particularly perturbed by recent proposals by Mostyn Estates to develop the Bodafon Fields which adjoin Craig y Don's Nant y Gamar Road. Just right of centre there is the original Washington Hotel, which protrudes 50 ft on to the promenade. Apart from being an unsightly obtrusion, it was also a traffic hazard as it caused a narrowing of the road at this point. In 1925 the building was demolished, and the new Washington Hotel built; this, with its lovely copper dome, is architecturally very pleasing.

The gracious landaus, stately carriages and the cart-horse wagons are gone now and have been replaced by the Model T, the Daimler and the like. The pace of life has quickened and the pollution is no longer a life-enhancing substance for cabbages and roses. The wide sweep of Mostyn Street is apparent here, but it would be a daring and foolish motorist who took the same route as this one up the street today; his journey would terminate after about one and a half yards. The milk cart on the left contains the familiar churns with the unhygienic milk-jug mode of transporting the liquid back to the kitchen.

Marks & Spencer opened in Mostyn Street in 1936. It was to undergo further extension in 1972, and later still in the 1990s. The building, though pleasant in itself as an example of modern architecture, caused some concern in that it did not entirely fit into its surroundings, which were buildings built to conform with the regulations established in the nineteenth century by the Improvement Commissioners.

In 1935, or thereabouts, house-building is progressing on the West Shore, later than elsewhere in the town. The boating pool for model boats, a hobby that seems to have died out, still receives its water from the Great Orme natural drainage system which flows through the old copper-mine workings. Glan y Don cottage in the foreground was the site of the one and only ship-building venture credited to Llandudno, the *Sarah Lloyd* having been built there in 1863.

The rock gardens in Happy Valley. These gardens were designed and developed by Pochin, who later worked on the more famous Bodnant Gardens just outside Llandudno. The adjacent Haulfre Gardens became a public park in 1929 when they were opened as such by David Lloyd George.

For many years the building that dominated the skyline in the Gloddaeth Street area was the Astra, a theatre, cinema and dance hall complex built in 1934. Two brothers from Rochdale built it at a cost of £70,000. At the opening, a telephone message was relayed from a Rochdale lass, Gracie Fields. The cinema part of the building was acquired by the Odeon Company, and consequently the building was known as either the Astra or the Odeon. For many years the theatre was the only one in North Wales big enough to meet the requirements of the Welsh National Opera Company, and they visited annually. Other major companies such as Carla Rosa, Sadler's Wells and the Gilbert and Sullivan D'Oyly Carte Opera Company also appeared there.

Lord Mostyn is opening the Colonnade leading to Happy Valley, March 1932. The structure cost £6,500 to build. The design was by one of Lord Mostyn's employees, Mr G.E. Humphreys, and the builder was Mr T. Ward. The town band are at the back of the crowd. A bricked-up doorway on the rock wall near the Colonnade used to lead to a wine cellar used by the Baths Hotel, which was demolished at the end of the nineteenth century.

Prince Edward Square now has an imposing feature, the War Memorial, an elegant obelisk crowned with the emblem of the Royal Welsh Fusiliers. On Remembrance Sunday each year crowds of ex-servicemen arrive from all over North Wales, and they hold a moving service. This photograph purports to be a record of the dedication of the War Memorial in 1922, which remembers the death of over 200 local men in the killing-fields of Flanders.

In 1933 David Lloyd George, the local MP, unveiled the White Rabbit Statue on the West Shore. The statue was designed and sculpted by a local monumental mason, Frederick W. Forrester, whose workplace was in Back Madoc Street. The inscription unveiled by Mr Lloyd George, and put there by the local council, shows a total disregard for historical accuracy. It reads, 'On this very shore during happy rambles with little Alice Liddell, Lewis Carroll was inspired to write that literary treasure Alice in Wonderland, which has charmed children for generations'. We have no proof that Lewis Carroll ever came to Llandudno – but equally we have no proof to the contrary.

In 1926 the North Wales coast said goodbye to *La Marguerite* and espoused a new love when the *St Tudno III* arrived in the same year. The *St Tudno* had a gross tonnage of 2,326 and could carry 2,493 passengers. She was built at Govan by the Fairfield Shipbuilding and Engineering Company. On her trips to the Anglesey coast she had to stop calling at Beaumaris and Bangor because of problems with manoeuvrability.

Five years after her arrival, the *St Tudno* was joined, in 1931, by her sister ship the *St Seiriol*, seen here off the Great Orme's Head. She was built by the same company and, in many respects was a smaller version of the *Tudno*. This vessel had a very distinguished Second World War career playing an important role in the evacuation of British troops from Dunkirk, receiving only superficial damage after seven return trips to the beach.

The baby of the company arrived in 1936. She was the *St Trillo*, originally called the *St Silio*. She was only 149 ft long and was licensed to carry just under 600 passengers. Here she is entering Amlwch harbour on her maiden voyage. Her two funnels look 'one too many' for a ship of her size, and indeed her forward funnel was a dummy. All the ships in the company were seconded for war service.

Seen here at Llandudno pier is the attractive little paddle-steamer *The Lady Orme* formerly *The Fusilier*. Her clipper bow and figurehead gave her an elegant line. She was not a large vessel. Owned by the Cambrian Shipping Company of Blackpool, and appearing on the North Wales coast in 1936, she ran excursions to Menai Bridge. She left for a while, and then returned in 1937, now owned by the Orme Cruising Company. She made a brief appearance again in 1938 but was broken up in 1939 after a 50-year career on the high seas.

The *Theodore Price* was launched for the last time on 22 October 1927 and was withdrawn from service in 1930. She was succeeded by two temporary boats: the *Sarah Jane Turner* which served for one year, and then the *Matthew Simpson* which served for 3 years.

The *Thomas and Annie Wade Richards* was the Llandudno lifeboat for twenty years, from 1933 to 1953. The boat cost £4,000. She was officially launched on Friday 28 September 1934, but had, before that, already saved six lives. She came with her own tractor which did much to alleviate the problems caused by having a lifeboat station so far from the shore. In all she was launched 57 times and saved 38 lives. The most tragic call-out was to the stricken submarine *Thetis* on 1 June 1939. The submarine had failed to surface after her first diving trial in Liverpool Bay fourteen miles from Llandudno. There were 103 men on board, and four managed to escape using the Davis apparatus. Ninety-nine men perished in this tragedy.

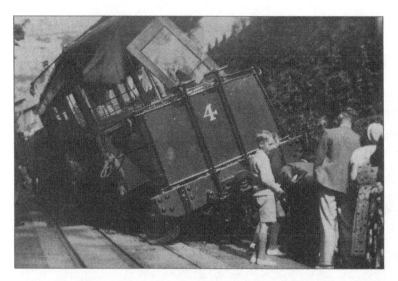

Disaster struck on the Great
Orme tramway on the 23 August
1932. Two people were killed, the
brakeman Edward Harris and a
12-year-old girl, Margaret
Worthington. A draw bar had
snapped, the brakes failed, and
the car left the rails and careered
into a wall. Coping stones from
the wall smashed through the
windows on to the defenceless
passengers. Fifteen people were
injured. The claims for damages
bankrupted the company but it
continued operating. In 1948, it
was bought by the town council.

The first fire brigade consisted of volunteer firemen equipped with several buckets, a hose and a ladder, and was formed
1854. In 1877 a horse-drawn Merryweather hand-pump was installed in a new building in Market Street. A steam pump
the *St Tudno* appeared in 1882. The first petrol-driven engine, seen here, came into service in 1925. The fire-chief is wearing
his First World War medals. The mascot is probably the son of one of the assembled firemen. A proud mother has spe
many hours making his miniature replica uniform.

In the years just before the Second World War Charles Wade's Concorde Follies or 'Gay Wayfarers', as they are called here, provided the entertainment in the Happy Valley Open Air Theatre. This elegant troupe performed song and dance acts interspersed with sophisticated comedic patter. The members of the troupe were: Charles Wade, V. Raye, Bob Howard, Bob Desmond, Primrose Hill, Edgar Morris, Madge Ward, Desmond O'Neill, Pat Dowers and Bobbie Burns. It was a mark of the times that so many people, along with stage-hands and others, could make a living from an open arena with deckchairs at about 3d each, 6d near the stage, and nothing on Aberdeen Hill.

The first May Day Celebration was held in the town in 1892 and they continued into the 1950s. In Llandudno the event, apart from its pagan origins, also meant the end of winter and the coming of the summer season with employment and money coming in. The celebration consisted of: parades through the streets with decorated floats, the crowning of a Carnival Queen, maypole dancing and street parties. This lovely tableau of 1932 is 'Britannia and her Court' with sailors and a lifeboat man. The trouble that has gone into making the costumes is a measure of the importance of the event.

21st Coast Battery RA Coast Artillery School, Llandudno, 1943. During the Second World War the armed forces arrived
Llandudno and the two Ormes became military zones. The government had transferred the Coast Artillery School from
Shoeburyness in Essex to North Wales in 1940. Llys Helig became a Coastal Artillery School in September 1940 and
1942 the Great Orme headland was seething with approximately 800 servicemen. A Wireless Officers' Cadet Course was
established and the summit hotel was requisitioned as a radar station. The hotel became government property and remained
so until after the war. The telephone communication facilities were also commandeered and played an essential role in the
wartime communication system. The remains of the observation posts and the foundations of the gun emplacements can
still be seen on the south-western shelf of the Great Orme and on the eastern side of the Little Orme.

During the Second World War the Imperial Hotel on the Promenade was the headquarters of Britain's Inland Revenue Service. The hotel was opened in 1872, and it came about as the result of merging several smaller boarding houses which had been built in 1865.

The Grand Theatre is seen here under construction in 1901, after many years of acrimonious debate in the town hall about its positioning and cost. During the war it became part of a decentralised British Broadcasting Company. Many well-loved wartime comedy series were broadcast from here. Catch-phrases such as: 'Can I do you now Sir?', 'Don't forget the diver' and 'This is Funf speaking' were heard in every home during the broadcast of the eagerly awaited ITMA programme with Tommy Handley. The author recalls the eager anticipation and the prayer that 'atmospherics', would not interfere. Sandy Powell asked, 'Can you hear me Mother?' from the same stage. The Grand Theatre was the original 'Happidrome'.

Known affectionately as 'Dad's Army', the Home Guard units throughout the country did a great deal to bolster the moral of the general population. They performed valuable ancillary services, in addition to their training as a last line of defence. They are frequently, unfairly, portrayed as a bumbling, badly equipped force, but most people who lived through the last 'War to End All Wars' (again) would gladly testify to their worth. This photograph, *c.* 1942, is believed to be of a Llandudno Home Guard Unit. There is a wide age-range in the assembled unit, and the presence of so many medals from previous conflict gives the lie to any suggestion that they were anything less than willing and able.

The 'City of Lincoln' allegedly the last flying Lancaster is accompanied by a Spitfire of the RAF's Battle of Britain Remembrance Flight over the Little Orme. This photograph will evoke memories of the Second World War.

During the Second World War the parlous state of the country meant that a great deal of war work was done by volunteers. The elderly, those with reserved occupations, and many women were drafted in to do this work, which they completed with an efficiency and a willingness that deserved the highest commendation. One such group is pictured here, *c.* 1943, in this rather poor quality photograph. It shows the Llandudno Voluntary Fire Service. Harrison's Coal and Coke Merchant has supplied the vehicle which towed the small trailer with main pump, hoses and stirrup pumps. The group's main purpose was to deal with minor fires which were started by the vicious little incendiary bombs which rained down to light up so many cities for a subsequent heavy bombing raid.

A group of American servicemen are enjoying 'R and R' (Rest and Recreation) in the 'Donut Dugout' in Vaughan Stree Llandudno. Towards the end of the war the Americans were stationed in the town, where they manned the gun emplacemen and took part in the work of the Artillery School. By 1942 the school was organised into a gunnery wing, wireless (Rada wing, coast battery, and administration and workshop wing.

This is the scene outside the Arcadia sometime in the 1940s. In the second row, and second from the left, is 'The Governor', Will Catlin. Since 1894 he had a busy life building a show business empire in Scarborough. He came to Llandudno in 1915, intending to take life more easily, but he was soon involved in show business here. He bought the ailing Hippodrome Skating Rink for £400 and almost completely rebuilt it. He named it the 'Arcadia'. His Pierrots were commanded to appear before Edward VII at Ruthin Castle, and thus his billing became 'Catlin's Royal Pierrots', only the second company to achieve that honour. The photograph below is a final curtain call at the Arcadia Theatre, taken at about the same time. It is clear that no expense was spared in clothing the elegantly attired cast. Included in the group are Jack Storey, Max and Maisie Norris, and Peter and Sam Sherry.

In 1948 a procession of almost regal proportions is coming along the Promenade. The star of the show is the leader the country rejected after the war, in the centre of this photograph. The epitome of British pugnacity, Sir Winston Churchill, is visiting the town on the occasion of the Conservative Party Conference of that year, held in the Pier Pavilion. Sir Winston stayed at the Grand Hotel and, according to Ivor Wynne Jones, he caused some consternation there when he requested a candle for room 109. None in the hotel, and the shops were shut, but somehow they managed to find several, and the icon of the twentieth century could light his cigars the way he liked to.

Changing Fortunes

Great Orme headland and Llandudno lighthouse from the air.

The summit complex was sold in 1952. It consisted of the hotel and 15 acres of land. It was bought by Mr L.T. Salts and h partner, the ex-World Champion boxer, Randolph Turpin. The price was £10,000. The building was completely renovate and modernised. The opening ceremony was conducted by the ex-World Flyweight Champion, Jimmy Wilde, and the crow turned up to mob the great boxers for their autographs. Unfortunately, Randolph Turpin ran out of luck. Mr Salts pulled o of the deal, and a lack of business acumen on the part of Turpin's advisers led to a bill for £16,000 from the tax-man. sold off everything he owned and returned to his native Leamington. He died prematurely in 1966, aged only thirty-seve The hotel was purchased later by Llandudno Urban District Council.

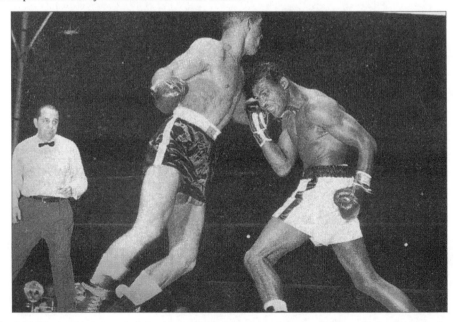

Randolph Turpin taking a punch during his world title fight against Sugar Ray Robinson (facing the camera).

This 1960 photograph marks the Golden Jubilee of the Llandudno Amateur Operatic Society, and the jubilee production was *The Gipsy Princess*. This light operatic society has for almost ninety years largely espoused a repertoire of Gilbert and Sullivan, with the occasional excursion into such as *The Student Prince*. In 1923 the Llandudno Musical Players formed a separate group, and the two companies, together with several noteworthy choral societies, now carry on the rich tradition of amateur musical production in the town.

Peter and Sam Sherry at the Arcadia in the 1950s. This type of entertainment, 'Acrobatic Violinists', was the type of music hall act that drew large numbers into the five or so theatres in the town. Llandudno was a rich entertainment centre during these postwar years, and a large proportion of the town's inhabitants was involved in show business. Alas no more! The visitors are in the hotels watching wide-screen television, something they could do just as well at home.

A traffic pattern is being established here in the 1950s and '60s which prevails to this day. The parked car is becoming the menace that it now is. In the top photograph a queue of people are waiting the arrival of tram 15, with traffic congestion on only one side of the road. Below, parked cars are on both sides of the road, and the best laid plans of the Improvement Commissioners for wide streets and easy traffic flow have come to grief. In 1999 the streets are permanently narrowed by a row of parked vehicles on both sides of the road, all day and every day.

There was considerable rivalry between the various bus companies in the area and the Llandudno Tramway Company. This rivalry was particularly acrimonious between the latter and the Crosville Bus Company. It was said that there would even be races between buses and trams to reach passenger queues first. This photograph from the early 1950s puts the protagonists into one frame. A Crosville owned Bristol Lodekka and tram No. 2 are on Bryn-y-Bia Road on Penrhyn Hill. After closure of the tram company in 1956 they tried to take the bus companies on at their own game. They set up a 'Red Bus' service, which staggered from crisis to crisis for several years. The last Red Bus ran into the Rhos Depot on Saturday 27 May 1961. This was soon followed by Crosville paying £40,000 for the goodwill of the tram company.

The demise of the tramway between Llandudno and Colwyn Bay is a good example of lack of foresight on the part of the authorities. The track obviously provided a valuable interlinking service and was an attraction for tourists. The company was starved of finance and could not face up to the competition from bus services and the private car. On the other hand it is easy to be wise after the event, and perhaps the shut-down was inevitable. In thirty years of service the system was estimated to have carried 130,000,000 passengers. Increased electricity costs and complaints about road congestion added fuel to the fire, and the above photograph was the result. No. 8, an open-topped double-decker, purchased in 1936 (ex-Bournemouth 16) was to be the last tram on the route. The driving was shared between Inspector Fred Wooley and a party of Bournemouth tram drivers. The date was 24 March 1956, a day on which hundreds of people took their last tram ride, shed a few tears, and sang 'Auld Lang Syne' outside the depot at Rhos-on-Sea.

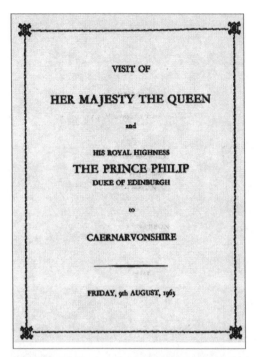

VISIT OF

HER MAJESTY THE QUEEN

and

HIS ROYAL HIGHNESS

THE PRINCE PHILIP
DUKE OF EDINBURGH

to

CAERNARVONSHIRE

FRIDAY, 9th AUGUST, 1963

On 9 August 1963 the Queen and Prince Philip visited the town as part of a general visit to Caernarfonshire. The visit coincided with the National Eisteddfod being held in Llandudno, and they visited the Eisteddfod site on Bodafon Fields. They went on to visit the boroughs of Conwy, Bangor, Caernarfon and Pwllheli. At Llanystumdwy they visited the grave of David Lloyd George.

he descendants of Miriam Jones of the cave are
nown as 'R'ogo' (literally 'from the cave') to this day.
he died aged 91 in 1910. The construction of the
arine Drive drove her from her home which was a
ave in the side of the Great Orme. Thirteen children
ere born and brought up in that cave. Her husband
onstructed wings of seagulls' feathers and string, and
ied to be one of the first man-powered fliers. He didn't
ucceed, and Mrs Jones had to nurse him back to
ealth. One of her descendants is seen here, Edward
oodey Jones, a well-loved and hardy character who
shed and provided trips around the bay. He died in
965. The town's feelings for Ted Yr Ogof were
xpressed in the memorial erected to his memory on
e promenade near the entrance to the pier.

THROUGH THIS MEMORIAL A BOATMAN'S HIGH IDEALS OF SERVICE LIVE ON
ERECTED BY PUBLIC SUBSCRIPTION
TO PERPETUATE THE MEMORY OF
EDWARD GOODEY JONES (TED YR OGOF)
WHO DIED NEAR THIS SPOT ON SUNDAY 20TH JUNE 1965, AGED 54

In May 1965 a new type of lifeboat arrived in Llandudno. The boats were known as ILB (Inshore Lifeboats) or 'D' class lifeboats. They were 15 ft 6 in long, built of neoprene proofed nylon and powered by a 40hp outboard motor. They were extremely manoeuvrable and were capable of 20 knots. They could be launched very easily and soon proved to be very useful for incidents, such as calls to yachts in distress, bathers in difficulty, or people stranded by the tide. They had the added advantage of only requiring a crew of one or two men. Since 1861 when the lifeboat station was opened in Llandudno the conventional boats have been launched 340 times and have saved a total of 237 lives. The inshore boats have, since 1965, been launched 516 times, and have saved 201 lives.

In living memory, and beyond, St Tudno's Church on the Great Orme has attracted thousands of worshippers to its open-air services throughout the summer season. The distinctive outdoor pulpit provides a modicum of shelter for the priest in what can sometimes be wild weather conditions. The feeling of being nearer one's maker outdoors must be the attraction for so many people who congregate to sing hymns and pray in this spectacular setting.

Mrs Eira Morgan made local history on 27 May 1966 when she was elected as the first lady Chairman of the Council (today she would have been Lady Mayoress). Aged sixty-six at the time, Mrs Morgan had been the only woman member of the council for the previous seven years. Mrs Morgan's family roots were firmly planted in the history of the town. Her great-grandfather had been a miller in the Nant-y-Gamar area. Her father had been a prominent solicitor, and her mother had taught in Lloyd Street School during the 1890s. She was the mother of two daughters and had five grandchildren, and her year of office was marked by her concern that the town should cater for the holiday needs of families with children. Some would say that this same concern needs to be reaffirmed today.

Civic Sunday was a very important day in the life of the council's chairman. It began with a church service and then a parade through the town. This was followed by a luncheon, and a speech from the chairman stating what the programme for the year would be. Mrs Morgan is accompanied by local dignitaries as the parade visits the Cenotaph on the Promenade.

Public subscription led to a nurses' and patients' chapel being built in Llandudno hospital in 1967. The chapel was interdenominational, and the dedication service was conducted by Dr D.D. Bartlett, the Lord Bishop of St Asaph, with senior representatives from all of the churches in the town. Mrs Eira Morgan, Chairman of Llandudno Council, is present, together with Miss M.E. Hughes, the hospital matron.

Mrs Morgan's successor as Chairman of the Council was a gentleman we have met before, Mr Bob Owen. Here he is, with h wife, being congratulated by Mrs Eira Morgan after his formal election to the post.

Above: In 1969 the big event in North Wales was the Investiture of Prince Charles as Prince of Wales at Caernarfon Castle. The day after the Investiture the Prince visited Llandudno where the crowds have gathered to greet him. The highlight of the festivities was a celebration pageant called 'Llandudno Regina – the Story of Llandudno told in Song, Music and Dance'. *Right:* the ladies of the Sewing Guild are preparing costumes for the pageant. They are, left to right, standing: Mrs R. Tingle, Miss J. Jones, Mrs N. Harvey, Mrs H. Smith, Mrs G. Lewis. Seated: Miss C. Davies, Mrs E. Ogle, Mrs E. Williams, Mrs E. Davies, Miss L. Childer.

The photograph above shows the Pier Orchestra in its heyday; the one below was taken on the occasion of the last conce conducted by Mr John Morava in 1974. He was hanging up his baton after 37 years on the pier. Mr Morava, in the white su is standing next to Robinson Cleaver, the impresario. In 1938, John Morava became the Musical Director of the Llandud Pier Company. In addition to his professional contributions, he gave freely of his time when the amateur musical life of t area required it. He played an important role in the productions of the Llandudno Operatic Society and the Colwyn Bay Choi Society. After his retirement music on the pier became a faint echo of its former self, and it soon ceased to exist altogether.

From the mid-1960s to the early '70s there was a popular move to raise funds to build a badly needed swimming pool in the town. It was felt that this would do much to alleviate the problem of too few indoor facilities for visitors. Eventually, on Friday 17 August 1972, the pool was opened by Councillor J. Treherne Willams, the chairman of the appropriate committee. In all, the townspeople and visitors raised £50,000 for the project. There is a commemorative clock in the foyer of the pool recognising his contribution.

In 1967 David Hughes opened his Antiquarian and Secondhand Bookshop in Madoc Street, Llandudno, and since then the shop has become a Mecca for book lovers all over the country. Mr Hughes, who is a native of Corwen, has a profound knowledge and a deep love of books. From this shop he sends books all over the world.

When the Zion English Baptist Church was demolished in 1967, because Mostyn Estates refused to renew its lease, the developers moved in and built the concrete boxes shown below in its place. This can only be called a very bad piece of design which would have appalled the Improvement Commissioners if they could have seen it. This eyesore remained in existence until the Victoria Centre was built to replace it.

new attraction was constructed in Llandudno in 1969, and on 30 June the longest cable-car system for passenger transportation in Great Britain was opened, another record for Llandudno, along with the longest funicular railway in Britain. The cabin lift starts at the Happy Valley and in just over a mile it reaches the summit station on an endless steel rope. It reaches 160 ft above ground over the former Great Orme Quarry, and, if you can stand heights, it offers spectacular views of Llandudno.

The visitor to Happy Valley may wonder about the significance of the large stone circle set in the green. Some residue of a prehistoric civilisation perhaps? The stones have been there since 1962, when they were set in preparation for the National Eisteddfod of 1963. Some of the rocks weigh over five tons. They are in place to mark the Druidic Gorsedd Ceremony, an essential and additional ingredient of all Eisteddfodau. The Eisteddfod of 1963 was held on Bodafon Fields, and was attended by Her Majesty the Queen and Prince Philip. The stone circle left from a previous Eisteddfod, of 1896, was later used to make a rockery in Haulfre Gardens, behind the existing stone circle. At the end of an Eisteddfod the site for the next venue is similarly marked.

The presence of snow in Llandudno is a relatively rare sight; the tempering effect of the Gulf Stream ensures a mild climate throughout the winter. There is snow here in 1967. The Gogarth Abbey Hotel is in the background, and, in the foreground, the absence of the White Rabbit Memorial shows that there has been yet another act of vandalism, and it has been sent for repair. Vandalism has been the scourge of this statue for the past sixty years. The steel cage which surrounds the statue currently presents no obstacles, and so the rabbit is without ears and the hand which holds the watch which informs the rabbit that he is 'late for a very important date' is missing. There were proposals to encase the statue in a reinforced glass box but, as usual, due to financial constraints, this cannot be done. At the moment it is a disgrace and the cost of repairs will probably far exceed the cost of adequate protection.

The breed of goat associated with Wales, as the regimental mascot of the Royal Welch Fusiliers, comes originally from Kashmir; Queen Victoria had been presented with breeding pairs by the Shah of Persia. They came by a circuitous route to Llandudno from Queen Victoria, who presented Sir Savage Mostyn with a pair from the royal herd in 1860. He kept them at Gloddaeth Hall and after a few years of breeding they became quite numerous, so he freed several pairs on the Great Orme. Not everyone regards them with affection, as they have a habit of leaving the slopes and paying their respects to nearby gardens. There was a cull some years ago which aroused a storm of protest. They are prone to disease and there could be problems associated with too close a pattern of inbreeding. They now have a warden who caters for their needs. The ones used by the Royal Welch Fusiliers are bred at Whipsnade, as an attempt to catch some during the First World War led to a 'death before dishonour' scenario as they leapt from the cliffs rather than suffer the indignity of capture.

Following the death of Will Catlin there was a
period when the Arcadia was run by his son, Bill
Catlin, and a consortium (1961–67). Then along
came Clive Stock and Robinson Cleaver, who made
Llandudno the entertainment centre of Wales
throughout the 1960s, '70s and '80s. Clive Stock
and his wife, Gwen Overton, seen here in 1960,
had illustrious singing careers on the West End
stage and Robinson Cleaver was a world-renowned
organist. At one and the same time they ran the
Arcadia, the Pier Pavilion, and the Sunday
concerts at the Astra. World class artistes such as
Howard Keele (seen below in April 1983) were
happy to come to Llandudno, confident that they
would be part of a first class production. Many
artistes were grateful for a start in show business
under the expert and friendly guidance of Mr
Stock and Mr Cleaver.

The end of the lighthouse occurred in 1973. The building had been there since 1862 after it was commissioned by the Mersey Docks and Harbour Board to cater for the needs of ships entering the Mersey and the Dee estuaries. It is a striking building, like a medieval castle guarding the area against seaborne invaders. Below its walls there is a 300 ft precipitous drop to the sea. In the front of the building there was a tower from which, in its heyday, a lamp of 18,000 candle-power flashed intermittently (every 12 seconds). It was visible as far as Snaefell on the Isle of Man, a distance of 54 miles. Today the lighthouse has retained its original striking external features, and is a guest-house. The original lamp is now in the Visitors' Centre on the Great Orme and, at the press of a button, it still works!

Alex Munro was the last of the Happy Valley Entertainers. He did much to keep the theatre alive in the Happy Valley. He ha a sharp wit and a consummate showman's flair. He could draw entertainment out of the most mediocre of circumstance He was good at getting people on to the stage, particularly children, and drawing out their talent, or lack of it! He was at b best when he was castigating the crowds on Aberdeen Hill who were bent on getting as much entertainment as possible fc the least expenditure. The picture below marks the end of The Happy Valley Shows; vandals have struck as usual, setting fi to the theatre, and nothing has replaced it.

A Period of
Challenge

The vestiges of earlier May Day celebrations occur each year in May when Llandudno holds its annual Victorian Extravaganza. The festival has been held for the past decade during the May Bank Holiday celebrations. The streets are full of fairground attractions, and entertainers. A steam traction engine rally coincides with it. Vast crowds of people attend every year. This view down Mostyn Street was taken from the big wheel.

In July 1979, by an amazing piece of good fortune, Mr John Jones of Llandudno Junction made one of the archaeological finds of the decade in North Wales; leaving his metal detector on while he went to 'spend a penny' led to a find estimated at £20,000. The bleeping machine led to the discovery of an ancient silver coin and, within minutes, Mr Jones had uncovered another sixteen. He contacted a friend, Mr Derek Blamire of Llanrhos, and they, together with Richard White of the Gwynedd Archaeological Trust, uncovered 200 Anglo-Saxon silver pennies. The coins dated from the reign of King Canute. They are now kept in the National Museum of Wales, Cardiff. Each coin is said to be worth approximately £100 to a collector.

The Aberconwy Centre was built adjoining the Arcadia in 1981, and was opened by Prince Charles with his new bride, Princess Diana. It was their first official duty after their honeymoon. Mr Clive Stock was the general manager of the centre until he left in 1987. It is a general-purpose building offering opportunities for a variety of sports and entertainment. The conference facilities are second to none, and it annually hosts national and international conferences. Above is Prince Charles at the opening of the centre, and below is Mr Stock and his staff on the day of his leaving.

The assembled staff of John Bright School (1981). The school had gone through a very busy transformation in the years prior to this. Originally the school was a selective grammar school named after its founder the great liberal reformer, John Bright. The school opened in 1907. Archer Thompson, one of Britain's most distinguished mountaineers, was the first headmaster. In 1987, after several difficult years of working on a split site, the newly formed comprehensive became a single unit on the Oxford Road site. An additional problem faced in those years was the implementation of the Gwynedd County Council's bilingual education policy, a reform which met with short-sighted disapproval by some parents. There is a pupil roll of 1,200 or so, and there are over 80 teaching staff. Among the assembled staff here are the headmaster, Gareth Jones, and senior staff: Howell Hughes, Howell Lloyd, Enfys Lloyd, Ifor Evans and Murray Thomas.

Hotels have been built on what was once a busy industrial complex with a copper-mine and Cornish beam engine. The Ty Gwyn Mine Company had been formed in 1835 to mine near what is now the Pier entrance. In 1855 the company closed down and the buildings were demolished, save for one chimney-stack which remained until 1969. A great deal of research by the Great Orme Exploration Society has led them to the mine entrance under the gardens near the Pier. Here are members of the Society at the opening of this entrance in 1986. Among the group are Dr Don Smith, Bob Smith, Councillor Tom Hannon, and the late Huw Tudno Williams. This was an exciting time for the society. There are plans for developing the area as a tourist attraction.

In 1987 a site near the half-way station on the Great Orme was surveyed with the intention of putting a much needed car park there. It was known that a considerable amount of copper mining had gone on in the vicinity in Victorian times. Within days it became clear that the supposed Victorian origin of the mine represented only a small part of the story. Stone and bone tools, and artifacts found there were subjected to carbon dating and produced amazing results. The mines were working at the same time as Stonehenge was being built, and 300 years before Tutankhamen was being entombed; 3,500 years of history had been discovered. It is not the biggest prehistoric mine in Europe, and probably not the oldest, but it is the oldest the public can get into, and is well worth a visit.

The Red Arrows sweep across Llandudno Bay in 1984.

There can be no doubting the fact that the Great Orme is an area of outstanding and magnificent natural beauty. The Vikings who saw the serpents' heads emerging from the sea mists and called them 'Worms' must have been as impressed as we are. In 1978 the Great Orme Country Park was formed, covering over 1,000 acres of the headland. There is not enough space in this book to describe fully the wealth of natural history that is contained within this relatively small space. An ornithologists' and botanists' paradise, a lot of the flora and fauna is unique to the Orme. The Visitors Centre, opened recently, is a well designed exhibition building, which contains exhibits to interest children of all ages.

Opened at the end of the 1980s, Llandudno's Ski Slope is situated near the Happy Valley. It is a slope which caters for all levels of skiing ability, and there is a Toboggan Run, which is a big attraction for non-skiers. At one time there was a proposal for a shorter cable-car to this area but unfortunately the plans fell through. The problem with the slope is road access through the Happy Valley Road, which is steep and very narrow. There is a stark utilitarian ugliness about the site that offends some people which could be obviated by some judicious tree planting.

In 1989 the Astra and Odeon Entertainment Centre was demolished. It had served the town well for 55 years. The theatre had been a venue for some of the world's greatest stars, including The Beatles and the Welsh National Opera. The removal of the 1,700 seat auditorium meant that large scale theatrical and operatic productions stopped coming to the town for the years between the demolition and the opening of the new North Wales Theatre in 1994. It also meant that a town once rich in theatrical opportunities was now down to one theatre on the Promenade, the Arcadia, and this, with one cinema, was not sufficient for the crowds of visitors to the town in the season. In 1999 it was announced that the remaining cinema, the Palladium, was to close permanently.

The current lifeboat is the *Andy Pierce*. She came on station in 1990 replacing the *Lily Wainwright*, which had been Llandudno for 26 years. The *Andy Pierce* has twice the speed of the *Lily Wainwright* with a top speed of 17 knots. She named after a legacy left to the Institute by Mr Andrew Pierce. She is a 12 metre 'Mersey' class self-righter and is powered two 280 hp Caterpillar 3208T diesel engines. She still has to be towed to the slipway by tractor.

A photograph from 1903 may seem out of place in this section, but the event pictured here has had repercussions in 1999. The photograph shows Lady Augusta Mostyn opening the lifeboat station in Lloyd Street. The station was situated half way between the two shores so that a decision by the coxswain would determine which shore to launch from when there was a call-out. Launching from the West Shore was discontinued when its sea defences were built. The problem now is that the RNLI wish to open a station on the North Shore promenade. There is a great deal of support for this, but there is equally support for a group of preservationists who wish to maintain the state of the Promenade in perpetuity, and they see this as the thin end of the wedge.

A disaster of immense proportions hit Llandudno in February 1994. There was no question that the best loved building in the town was the listed Pier Pavilion, and now it was being destroyed by fire. This building had been purchased some years earlier by a developer who did anything but develop it. It was slowly decaying and falling to pieces as the weather took its toll. The glow in the sky sent the author scurrying into the bitterly cold east wind, equipped with camera to record the scene. Hundreds of people came out to watch the disaster, shake their heads in disbelief, and applaud the work done by the fire services from all over North Wales to stop the fire spreading to nearby hotels.

After the fire a fireman is damping down the smouldering embers. Some say the building had been occupied by squatters for some time, and others reported that they had seen children running from the scene shortly before the fire began. No one knows how it was caused.

All that is left is the distinctive wrought-iron front of the Pavilion. It was some sort of a miracle that the fire did not spread to the surrounding hotels. The Grand Hotel was particularly vulnerable because of its proximity. Nothing could be saved, despite a careful survey of the ruins.

The awful hole left after the fire is still here after 5½ years.

In 1994 the theatrical and artistic life of Llandudno took a distinct turn for the very much better after years of theatre closures and general cultural malaise. In that year the North Wales Theatre opened and provided the town with a facility which is, perhaps, unrivalled in Wales. The external appearance adds an air of distinction to what had been a rather drab stretch of sea-frontage. Proposals for the future development of this site offer exciting prospects.

The interior is simply breathtaking. There is a 1,500 seat auditorium facing one of the largest and best equipped stages in Great Britain. Very few theatres in the country offer programmes of such variety and scope. In all there are some 340 performances a year, ranging from the Welsh National Opera's Wagner through International Ballet, National Orchestra, West End Shows to one-man stand-up comedy. The popularity of the venue is proved by the fact that each year some 200,000 tickets are sold. In conjunction with the Aberconwy Centre, which it adjoins, it makes a magnificent Conference Centre offering world class facilities. *Below:* A Welsh National Opera production at the North Wales Theatre.

Llandudno's Victoria Centre was opened on 7 July 1992 by Mr Joseph Edge, the General Manager. It has subsequently been developed through two further phases. Every month over a quarter of a million people visit the centre, and over 15,000 cars use the car park each month. Originally part of the Sun Life Properties Company, it is now part of the Richard Ellis St Quintin Group. Architecturally, the building is a pleasant addition to Mostyn Street, and is a vast improvement on what stood there before.

One of the worst disasters to hit Llandudno in living memory occurred on 10 June 1993. The heavens opened and 5½ inches of rain fell in 3½ hours. The town's sewage and drainage system could not cope. People sitting and watching television or having an evening meal, suddenly became aware that their carpets were floating, and the suddenness and the severity of the flood gave them no time to save their homes. The town has, over the years, put up with sea-flooding when high tides and adverse winds occur together, but this was something entirely foreign to the town's experience. The repercussions were dreadful for many people who lost everything, and had to wait many months before they could return to their homes. A great deal of damage was done to the Great Orme, as rain-loosened soil formed a slurry which brought rocks crashing down on to Marine Drive, as seen below.

There had been a gasometer on this site in Maesdu Road since the first was installed in the mid-nineteenth century. The gasometers had always been the biggest in North Wales. This one being demolished in 1994 was capable of holding 1,000,000 cubic feet of gas. It was the third and last gasometer to be built here. For many years it was fed by natural gas from the North Sea. In the Maesdu area, which might be regarded as Llandudno's industrial area, there was an incinerator and steam turbine for generating electricity and there was also the chimney of the Llandudno Brick Works.

In 1989, a Southern Railway Clan Line, Merchant Navy Class Pacific is standing in Llandudno Station. It was the first stea[m] engine to visit the town since the demise of steam on the line. The train had come from Crewe to Llandudno Junction und[er] steam and then on to Llandudno under steam. Because there were no facilities for turning the engine, the train had to [be] pulled back to Llandudno Junction by diesel locomotive and it proceeded from there to Holyhead under steam once mor[e]. Below, the engine is arriving in Llandudno Junction to pick up the rest of the train.

areth Jones AM, OBE is a native of Blaenau Ffestiniog. He
raduated with honours from Swansea University, and
ught for several years before becoming Deputy Principal of
e newly opened Snowdonia National Park Study Centre at
laentwrog. He became Headmaster at Ysgol John Bright,
landudno in 1975. He was responsible for unifying a split
te comprehensive school on to a single site, and for
mplementing a bilingual education policy. In 1991 he was
warded the OBE for his services to education. In 1997 he
as elected as a County Councillor. In May 1999 he topped
e poll in the National Assembly election. This was a
istoric victory for a popular man of the highest integrity
nd reputation.

Mrs Betty Williams, AS/MP, has been the Labour Member for
Conwy since the landslide victory for Labour in 1997. Before
entering Parliament she had a very active career in local
politics, including being the Mayor of Arfon Borough
Council. She is a Member of the Welsh Affairs Select
Committee. She is particularly interested in consumer affairs,
rail transport, special education and health issues. With her
North Wales colleagues she has fought hard and successfully
to achieve Objective 1 status for North Wales. She has
expressed a great interest in the development of Llandudno
Hospital, and she is an ardent supporter of the work being
done at St David's Hospice. She has long been associated with
Special Education provision at Ysgol Gogarth Llandudno.

The Right Honourable Lord Roberts of Conway, robed for his introduction to the House of Lords as a Life Peer in October 1997. Before his elevation Wyn Roberts was Conservative MP for the Conwy Constituency, which includes Llandudno. He represented the constituency for 27 years from 1970, when he won the seat from Labour, to his retirement in 1997. He was, from 1979 to 1994, a Minister at the Welsh Office. This 15-year period was a record for length of service in the same Department of State. He was knighted in 1990, and became a member of the Privy Council in 1991. He was the Minister responsible for Health in Wales, and as such he was deeply committed to the preservation and enhancement of Llandudno Hospital, and a number of major improvements were carried out during his period of office. He played a key role in the development and upgrading of the A55 and the building of the Colcon sections, which included the Conway Tunnel opened by Her Majesty the Queen in 1991.

The leading Liberal Democrat in North Wales is unquestionably the Reverend Roger Roberts of Llandudno, seen here with the then leader of the Liberal Democrats Paddy Ashdown. Mr Roberts, a Superintendent Methodist Minister, was brought up in Llanrwst and Conwy, and was educated at John Bright Grammar School, Llandudno, Bangor University and Handsworth College, Birmingham. He is a familiar face on television, and is a regular presenter of Radio 2's *Pause for Thought*. His work for humanitarian relief receives international recognition. He organised the Wales Ethiopia Ambulance Campaign, and water lifeline projects to Rwanda and Kurdish Refugees. Recently he has been campaigning vigorously for sending water purification plants to Kosova. He is Wales' representative on the Council of European Liberals.

In 1999 Llandudno's first piece of commissioned art for 70 years was unveiled by Dafydd Parry-Jones, the chairman of Conwy County Borough, in the refurbished North-Western Gardens. The piece, designed by Craig and Mary Matthews of CAMM Design, New Brighton, Wirral, cost £20,000 and is a hexagonal column 5 metres high. Panels on the column depict scenes from the town's history including a copper miner, a tram, and shop fronts. The whole is topped by a queen's crown of fish and sailing boats. At night it has a Belisha-style lamp which is reminiscent of a lighthouse. The column is made of steel, bronze and stone, and has been coated with corrosion resistant resin. The column was chosen by the public from seven possible designs submitted to mark the millennium.

The eclipse of the sun over Llandudno Bay, 11 August 1999.

Acknowledgements and Picture Credits

With special thanks to five friends whose generosity made this book possible: Derek Blamire, Bill Oliver, Glyn Morris, Tom Parry and David Haynes.

Thanks are also due to the following people who helped in its preparation: Roger Brown ARPS, Naomi Broomfield, Margot Catlin, Mike Day, Geoff Ellis, David Hughes, Bryan Hurst, Mike Hitches, Gareth Jones AM, Harvey Lloyd, Jim Lowe ARPS, John Lawson Reay, Freda Mealings, Andrew Morley, Sue Morley, John Mowlem and Co., PLC, John Murgatroyd, Huw Roberts, Peter Roberts, Roger Roberts, the Right Hon. Lord Roberts of Conway, Clive Stock, Betty Williams MP, Llandudno Historical Society, and the patient staff of Llandudno Library.

Authors consulted were: Ivor Wynne Jones, Michael Senior, F. Ron Williams, Aled Eames, John Cowell, Don Smith, Keith Turner, Eifion W. Roberts, Mike Hitches, Mary Aris and Ian Skidmore.